WAITING IN THE WINGS

by

Muhammad Rafique Farooqi

COPYRIGHT 2022 @ WAITING IN THE WINGS
By Dr. Muhammad Rafique Farooqi

Edited by Marie Ezekiel
Arranged by Tess Ritumalta

ISBN:
Softbound/Paperback-978-621-470-253-4
Hardbound-978-621-470-254-1
MOBI/KINDLE-978-621-470-255-8

Published by:
Poetry Planet Book Publishing House
Rosario, Pozorrubio, Pangasinan, Philippines
Contact Number: 09554960094
Email: maritesritumalta@gmail.com

This book is dedicated to my readers, without their attention all my endeavors are void.

PREFACE

Poetry is an art of genius which speaks powerfully and inclusively when it assumes its connections in the modest enclave of time and space for purpose of attracting attention and provoking an emotional response.

In the blessed lifetime, it emulates a desire, a struggle, and a survival to create dreams becoming an incentive to feel eternity in dreamed heavens. Numerous skies expose reality, infinity, eternity, and integrity nourishing our grey matter sparkling to know the invisible axis of existence.

Life will end, time not end. We are part of the universe. Our souls get energy from love. If you have lost your love, find yourself in yourself. We face injustice, betrayal, deception cruelty, and learn to live. Just know how to stand strong.

With due respects,

Dr.Muhammad Rafique Farooqi

TABLE OF CONTENTS

I AM LOVE

I am love,
See me in your eyes,
I am an image of the sensations,
Close your eyes,
I am still there,
Can you feel me,
This is a glow,
Now you know,
Brightness tears the darkness,
 To see the dust of our,
Motherland,
The soil smells the roses,
fossiled in eternity,
and sea waters germinate the pearls,
and gives clouds to the sky,
and becomes snow on mountains,
I am core heat of your life,
and glow on your face.
white doves flutter,
in my rhyme.
keep me on your lips,
I will smile in your arms.

I AM WITH YOU

Sunlight comes from different angles,

 it comes from the same sun,

I am different from you in some respects,

but I am certain to be with you.

I STAND ALONE

I stand alone
With my warm zeal to unfold
When his soul is tired of its own
I speak words
source of solace
I pray out loud
For conviction of betrayal
For the revenge to be quenched
And savory to be the best taste
Unless you wave your sword
And behead your desire
And kneel to worship
your bluntness astounds me
A paramount of psychosis
Reminds me of natives of this land
Their voices became echoes
their screams are fossils
Buried under the concrete of your cities
How you can wave flags of peace
When their graves are unseen
While the wave of anger will crash every sunrise.

IN THE LIGHT OF FULL MOON

On your wet lips,
rose water shines,
In the moonlight,
that giving soft shadows,
spreads up to horizons,
and stars are shy to flicker,
before moon,
sea waters are still and sleeping,
distant Iceland,
disappearing in the lap,
of the sea,
serene notes of rhyme floating,
with swift moves of your fingers on strings,
my dreamy thoughts lost in your,
blue eyes,
It keeps me still with breaths,
and spikes of beating pacemaker,
and growing beauties of heavens,
touch my shoulders with,
the warmth of breaths,
love makes me talk,
to feel and to move,
an essence of existence,
love is the water of heavens,
and soul wetting her lips,
to intake the heavenly blessings.

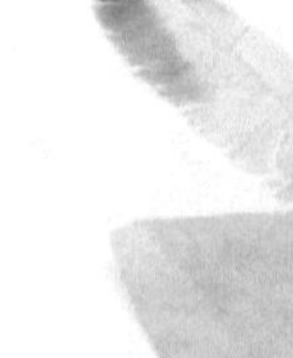

INDEPENDENCE DAY

With green soft,
and delicate leaves,
 my little friend,
waiting for my caressing,
and watering,
with smiling gaze,
happy in his container,
blooming with friendly nurture,
I think this place is not better,
for him,
he needs,
soft fertile soil in the ground,
I loved him in my own way,
but he is capable of going on,
with his own way,
today is his independence day,
standing proudly,
In his soils,
breathing and smiling,
over his independence.

INSOMNIAC OTHERWISE

Dark evils roaring In fields,
War does not end,
Swords shine with ego,
Sun blazing the sands,
episcopal hates and revenge,
Cultivated beyond civilization,
to get fed by blood,
Sky staring with anger,
Red storms to blow overall,
Never on the price of fate,
Death leaves no pulse,
Eagle soars with the sun,
Thirst chokes the breath,
Mirage shines like a river,
Dawn opens the eye,
I am alone and hated,
Sands drifting in eyes.

JUST SMILE FOR ME

Mine inner weathers,
get changed with your faces,
your sorrows,
are my autumn,
my journeys through,
the falling leaves of autumn,
with my anemic face of withering leaves,
and your smiles,
are raindrops in deserts,
your tears are suffocating summer,
that burns my soul.
and you gladly smile,
are a harbinger of springs,
and fragrance of a flower,
 in my mind,
you are my soul,
and my flow of,
my blood,
with a beating heart.

.

KNOW IT BETTER

The dream was not bad not good
not sad sleepy eyes
wandering in the bedroom
raising supple twig above the face,
some mantra murmured
beneath lips tea, not wine
closed eyes impulsive thoughts
 sorting puttees
wrapping on thighs wanderlust
horse strides phone call not yet
amazing thought

LEGACY AND UPRISE OF PIRACY

My ambition that becomes my sword
I dwell in mysteries
That cast shadows on the face of pain
Let me succeed beyond pains
On swollen grounds
Looking with my hawk eyes
Preserving spears in saddlebags.
To begin
A journey of a warrior
Emerged from untold tales
Like redemption of
crewed sailing to endless
I barely stand for that
What was never a sacred belief
The resurrection of a lost civilization
From crippled bones of natives
With ghost faces
Barely standing upright
Dressed like spooky pirates
For the most doors of hell
Stand open
Let's give them a way
Dust rises far away

LET ME GO

Warm the chilled airs,
with burning bones,
and smelling dead lizard,
 open to roots,
eyeballs pungently blinked,
to know,
the wayside exits.
weathers pleased on the way,
pinching memories with toothed fingers,

LET US DREAM TOGETHER

Even we can't,
walk and breathe together,
we can dream together,
and cross every line,
which stops us,
from the nurture of our love,
Just smile,
like a rose opening,
his petals,
and have a soulful flight,
coming from depths,
of the horizon, and blue sky,
being kind to us,
makes everything blue.
and haze vanishing,
In the presence of brightness of love.

LIFE

We have been a creature,
frail and faulty natured
finding nothing dearer and wiser
Linger on
Loves lost in silence.
A frustration to round up
With Longing soul
That withers in winters
Decline in weather
Did not find the path
Right-to-door
The passion wiped in the mist and fog
journey of life staggers on
Unpaved roads Suffering bumps
Tasting the ups and downs
And we endow
Miser engraved on the face of wrinkles
Withered leaf of life rolling with
Thrusts of the wind
Efforts to reduce
The burden of life
On Paining shoulders

LIFE TO LIVE

Life is not some kind of suave,
debonair blessed type,
I am to ask some questions from me,
what does a hot thing like,
in a man who walks around,
with his shirttail hanging out,
and his cereal bowl full of chili,
there may be a hundred reasons
to live with stilling perils,
even with cool cat killers,
and charmingly cynical vowing
to blow us in stone ages,
but hopes always not with struggles,
under the bitter curve of the tongue,
pouring out some sweet liquid.
and the sky changes colors,
not asking us,
our footprints on sands of life,
 telling our path,
while death runs faster than life,
and standing on the victory stand,
before we reach the finish line.
chewing our warm flesh.

LOAD SHEDDING

When the boat is endangered,
to sink,
some luggage is dropped off in the waters,
my feet are getting heavier,
and swollen,
in the journey of life,
what my companions,
feel better,
they must do,
it remains a long distance,
to go with,
I hope nothing,
but a drop.

LOVE AT LARGE

Like a lurid love letter,
provoking to tears,
feeling you,
someone at large,
meeting in secrete could be sensitive,
a litany of horror,
while I have a heart,
I never lose it,
in this maudlin world,
badly sentimental,
over crises,
to know someone good,
with oodles of silly souls,
everyone on a leash,
 I can linger on a bit,
on things bitterly familiar,
but we love,
a good mystery,
that keeps in this world breathing,
revel in being mindful of things,
that wants us to bling.

LOVED

Touch my soul with,
your blue lake eyes,
from beyond the vision,
of heavens,
I am walking on the road,
paved with rose petals.
and snow on my eyebrows,
waiting to melt with,
the glow of your cheeks.
Come down from the clouds,
like fairy of dreams.
just becoming the rain,
on my skin.
my heartbeats,
on each and every recite,
of your name,
come my soul with each,
and every dream,
making the nights,
blinks of cool and silent sky.

MIGHT IN SIGHTSEEING

I am born..to...
.............die
and blessed with a time period,
to live,
in between,
a life desire,
a struggle,
a survival,
to create dreams,
in rapid eye movement sleep,
an incentive,
 to feel eternity,
in my dreamy heavens,
numerous skies,
to expose,
the reality,
 infinity,
integrity,
grey matter sparkling,
to know,
provoked to break
perplexing notes
of vanished,
translucent,
invincible,
invisible axis of existence,
dormant hidden, truths,

with escaping velocities,
orbital relations,
 inertial sickness,
centripetal forces,
to leave behind the ancestors.
accepting the drifted,
weightlessness,
floating in rhythmical blinks.
somewhere in love with brightness,
heavenly vision,
in all chromic spectra,
the cosmic realities,
 above visions,
what my tissues can mount,
with my will,
just time is about,
to get, over,
I am to be replaced.
 but I will go on loving,
whomever to love,
the angles prey bowing,
and respectful to this span.
I was blessed,
it is my vision,
 and his might.
everything bright,
my heart my mind,
I am ever to love,

MIRAGE

For my destiny,
with my blistered feet,
on the unfriendly desert,
I went on,
breaking up in pieces,
that was just a mirage,
all my efforts,
vanished in a mirage.

MISADVENTURES

The days and nights are worn away
to endure bitterly provoked despair with fear from
darkened nights
one more wound is to bleed tearfully,
your invincible reluctance
wins all the wars by the unfairness
this was the last deal by standing on lies
celebrating concern of joined conspiracy
with failure of temperaments of outrage
willing to pay the price
of outward gratification
and shouting the loudest slogans to impose their will
suffered demise of courage and morals in dismay.

MISTAKEN

It was me mistaken you
it was not your fault
otherwise, just know this
you play
and break hearts a sin
never punished ever
but time lapses
any regret and neglects
any misfortune just come
and see
how the worse is done.

MISUNDERSTANDING

I will be unable to stop,
with my little hands,
the wall intended,
to fall over me,
and the storm,
to overrun me,
my little eyes blink to close,
while pungent smokes
that is to blur my mind.
there is one reality,
that hangs like a dagger,
on the tip of the nose,
that you becoming different,
day by day,
It breaks my innermost silence,
and tranquility,

MOONRISE

As I am painting,
your hands in full moonlight,
a dream is played,
in my sleep,
and stars are shining in your eyes,
I am lost in some,
deep valleys,
as a smile is born on your face,
my heartbeats are voluminous,
 love fills desires with copious fragrances.,
a curl of hair runs on your cheek,
my heart dances like a boat in the,
deep waters,

MY LOVE IS FADING IN

In the dark, all around,
a journey with,
eyes widely open,
and pupil's whole dilated,
the dark trees,
parting clearer and clearer,
the stars vanished slowly,
while the sky became grey,
and brightened love,
slowly fading in,
my love is converging in my whole,
and it is spreading in life everywhere,
in the smile of the baby,
in the ripple of waters,
in the fragrance, of flowers,
in the eyes of waiting beloved,
in the veins of roses,
in the colors of the rainbow,
in the rhythm of dancing strings,
in the melody of a song,
in the beauty of face,
in the warmth of sunshine,
in the Lapland of dawn,
my love is fading in,
my love is my brightness.

MY SOUL

While I think of dreams,

lingering in my mind,

I see you in extremes of delicacy,

of thoughts,

fragrance and colors,

of your smiles sparkling before my eyes,

while a ripple of smiles,

moves from the rose petals,

of your lips to the horizons,

of my imaginations giving life touches,

to my heart and mind,

and your soft-minded gestures,

give peace to my visions,

when I want to paint you,

the canvas of vision extends to the heavens.

I feel eternal existence in me.

MY SOUL NEEDS A FACE

I am going from my home,
wherever I am to go,
I will be back to my home,
I will need it.,
to be at home.
or it will be my dream to be at home,
if I am unable to return.
it is part of my life.
it is my soul,
that needs a structure,
a face to be someone,
my soul needs me,
to be someone,
my soul needs my face.
To face life.

NATURED. ALL

Let him sting me...

it is his nature.......

let me save him...

it is my nature......

a little poor scorpion

NIGHTMARE

Unstable ambitions,
and dreams erected,
in mists,
shattering into icy grains,
drifting before eyes,
and vistas of vested,
dreamland carved in image,
rendered subtle to existing,
Peevish thoughts,
Preverted sensations,
causing numbness to cry painfully.
and night is heavy this time,
On breaths,
and swim for survival,
Landing on bare skin,
seeming distant echoes,
to an unknown fate.

NIGHTMARE FANTASIES

The nightmare is just,
to kiss my eyes,
while I am sleeping,
no one dies.
you can kill me,
every midnight,
lambs are innocent,
hold your knife,
I am just on my way,
come on baby,
never say,
 none is my friend,
life is just to end.
I am here,
come anyway,
just to stay,
no other way.

NOT ON OTHER DAY

My heart is like a sick bird,
hiding in his wings.
And life is becoming hard,
like climbing on the tree,
with wheezing asthma,
You deserted me
like a running piece of cloud,
leaving me alone.
I am feeling this,
like an amputated leg
giving false perception
of its painful presence.
I have become just like a shadow
which is not part of any matter,
my not ever at now,
nor at on other days.

NOW & THEN

At times we did not collect

what we are going to recollect now.

Anyhow

Our passion shines

Still

We have motives

To drag passions

On searing sands.

ON THAT EVENING

Once we were,
breathing,
smiling,
and living,
on the same,
and things became,
strange on some tornado,
we could not find,
our loves,
our homes,
in wreaked jetsam,
and to seek the straws,
of dry jungle grasses,
to refurbish our nest,
and loneliest cries.
shadowed long,
when the days were over.
with bloodsheds.

ONE CUP OF TEA.....NEVER TO CRY

I am all alone,

in the crowded street,

hiding myself by closing my eyes,

closing my ears,

feeling nothing,

a deceptive escape,

with inner mingled,

sickness,

to keep alone,

just wanting one leaf of the spring,

season,

one color of the rainbow,

hiding in my raincoat,

from one drop of the rain.

the purity of elements,

symbolic texture,

the rhythm of latched desires,

an integral part of solemn life,

the heat of life,

endowed to love,

nothing else,

it is me for peace.

OTHER EYES

I can see you
when I close my eyes
when I rest on a log or tree,
in the open sky,
and you know my sensations
and my all blossoms,
and my old fascination
I'll not let you go,
I'll hold you in my dreams

OVER THE TROUBLES

This was all,
pretense about,
the sovereign visions,
that claimed the truths,
in invited grimly, gestures,
bound to wall-to-wall,
with bones and blood.
some vowed to rumble,
the paining heads,
and no claim on dusks,
and dawns,
born perceptible approaches,
of blind hands,
seeking,
streets and faces stained with sins.
the wayward feuds reluctant to pin the eyeball,
over the walls,
this whole staged troubled zones.,
bounded to quite their throats.
and once again to the will,
and day robbers joined to rule.
this advance in peril,
fill the flaws of earth,
with their dead bodies.
and war fields are clear,
to see the next war of generations

PAINFUL ENDS

In the end,
eagers and excitements,
find flaccid tongues,
Achieved or lost,
dribble on the feet.
The inner and outer wars,
bring vultures, to eat,
dead aims,
and ill-smelling,
blood of realities,
gets served to flies of lies.
The long hands of time,
bend the spines of arrogance.
the withered leaves of autumn,
fuel the smoke and fire of demolition.
choices to life and death,
written on the ill-fitted shoes of miseries,
which blister the feet
of the warriors and rust, the shines,
of swords of ages.
Ends are always painful.

PRINCE LIVING UNDER A TREE

I am with nothing,
and want nothing more,
I am living under a tree,
and dreaming heavens,
I lost my hunger,
after three episodes of hunger pains,
I take pleasant showers,
in open rains,

PROMISED GENES

It is solemnly endowed,
promised inheritance,
encoded genetically,
red roses,
and butterflies,
and green leaves,
are miracles of beating hearts,
and sunsets,
rising moons,
and glimpses of silver mountains,
with clicked gestures,
of silversmith,
cutting the flesh of events, to bones,
and you are a familiar face of the time,
what you know about,
someone in front of you,
and light spotting your face,
and cutting the darkness,
like dagger,
and walls standing like hills,
and pictures of fates,
mounted with dust,
and blow of wind revealing,
eyes of primitive man.
and on recollection,
of evidence,
like a bird,

refurbishing his nest,
a man stands straight,
on his two limbs,
and
amazed over this re-evolution.

RATHER TO LIVE WITH HARASSMENT

I remained unable to,
.find myself,
since I got lost,
and the shadow of me,
disappeared with sunset.,
blending with the prevailing darkness,
and the core of my visions,
is like a distant star flickering,
with a density of chilled winds,
I am to put my favors,
on my worn eyes.,
and the feebly breathing soul,
lurking in a stagnant pool of mind,
and I am drifting myself,
lapsing in intermediary circling,
endeavored life,
my enemy is sharp,
and vigilant,
and reluctant to know,
my whereabouts,
but I don't know,
where I am,
since the day I got lost.

REASON TO FEAR

The midnight howls,
crying over the,
pyramids of Pharaoh,
unable to fill the Nile with their tears,
and brittle skins snapped,
by urban adventures,
in unknown crypts,
lying underground bones.
history flows like,
a galaxy in the universe,
a thousand suns heating,
the frozen realities,
and gushed rivers,
feeding the deserts,
of thirst,
and blood flow in the.
veins of the sky,
vital for love and eternity.,
and one slogan,
of one voice,
to clear the darkened clouds,
below the foundations,
of willful thoughts,
bringing imagery,
of existence.

REASON TO LIVE MORE

Why you have left your power to dream
as the shadow follows your footsteps
I remember standing in the courtyard
looking at the cleft in the wall
I painted my figure on the wall
with the black of my own ashes
I lost the count of time
and met the last dead man in the dream
he was still trying to have my garden
but like the wise, I broke my dream
whence my mindless masters
have sent me
now I am looking at my feet and realizing
this me all weepy
with some reason to live more

REFURBISHED......FOR LOVE

No dream retreats,
from its orientations,
no limits, no boundaries,
can bound reals and dreams,
dreams never get old,
an old guy can also be a dream,
of fairyland,
a dream of a young one.,
tummy tucking,
acrylic teeth,
intraocular lenses,
botulism toxin injection,
removal of wrinkles,
hair transplantation,
restores all that is gone,
Viagra and vitamin E;
can make him a gladiator,
thus old man, refurbished.....
for new love.
and new home,
new car.

.stormcaller. Apr 25,2009

RISING BACK TO LIFE

Like rising from the deep waters,
from high compression of waters,
like a sea diver with untidy breaths.
 having disarray in thoughts,
by a marked disorder of fears.
hiding like a guilty-faced,
on the hind line of the crowd.
just like painful hope in the dark,
with blind eyes in thunder and spark,
with a spell of forgetfulness,
anxious and waiting,
depressions more poignant,
dim and half vision,
breed from chills,
rising back to life,
from depths of forgetfulness.
hopeful again,
coming back to you,
...........again.

RIVALS ON RUN

Scratch in the imagination,
spreading in random,
the opaque direction of visionary,
planes particular to the end finding love,
in longing arms of cherry-faced monsters,
eating foul smelled fungus,
recipes in ugly bowls of gravity,
all crystal ware shattered to whirling storm grinding,
rusted walls of existence,
shines in new horizons,
blinding the eyes.
and evils melted into wax,
like vomits,
bile running in the streets of,
dirt made castles.
marking the history,
with the sharpness of revengeful swords,
dissecting the reality,
up to lower ends,
the final dual on the,
other century awaiting the rivals.

ROADSIDE SPELLS

The road of the life,
extends,
with bends,
we bear,
the fate, sooner,
or late,
we find love,
or some hate,
and some other conditions,
some doubts,
some suspicions,
some beliefs,
some deviations,
when we take this road,
with evens,
or odds, we weave,
stories of a miser,
and joy,
and of some,
different,
we wonder it more,
when we find some corner,
like rejected toys.

SANDS & FLIGHT

Thoughts broken,
into sands,
a fist of diamond sand,
losing every second,
flames of turmoil,
dancing and whirling,
in directions,
tears of dew,
alive in hopes,
inhaling smokes deep,
poisoning blood,
roadside tree running back,
mirage of deserting running,
far and beyond visibility,
the window of thoughts,
broken by diamond crystal,
and soul torturing image,
nightmarish kisses of,
furious ignitions of sparks,
a bird flight,
in the night, long to go,
never back,
around and proximate,
cave of huge cut-throat.

SAY SOMETHING FOR ME

Let me see in the darkness
Let my dream and nightmare
Stroll in the depths of forests
Silence whirls to break
What the creature of dark learns for me
Even my desire dies slowly
I still exist in the depths of solitude
I sip fallen tears
Memories run like a thorn bush
Can you say something for me
Something peering
And lucid
So if you wake up in the morning
You find me nowhere
Not in your dream
Nor in your nightmare.

SCARS

Writing some words,
erasing some words,
making lines,
straight and curved,
bizarre
A figure of weird
Dejected and turned down
I feel amused to win
all the lost wars
With default conspiracy
Crept a way to figure out
Invincible fronts
getting long scar
on the face of the history
Pissed like frontline of
Anti-terror campaign
I find myself short of ethics
Glancing up and down
Draw a circle around me
fighting unpopular wars
I feel prisoned
powerfully in the dark ages

SELF EXILE

I looked last time,
the barren walls of,
my inner city,
a torn dirty banner,
hanging on,
with window,
I lived there with my loneliness.
a self-exile,
but painfully,
I refrained to adore,
and from existence.
walking bare hand again,
on the road of life,
that ends on an endless path.

SELF TALKING

I have to tell,
my friends a lot,
but they have no time for me to listen,
they are busy in,
talking about,
new cars,
forecasting forex rates,
and obliging,
new beautiful,
assistant to of boss,
I am to tell my sufferings to myself,
and busy biting my nails,
scratching line,
on painted walls,
stripping threads from my shirt,
crushing lead pencil,
with my canines,
looking into the mirror,
again and again,
my therapist,
getting,
hopeless,
and going to declare me,
a self-talking person like,
a third-degree burn.

SHADOWS OF YOUR SOUL

I listen to your voices,
you are never here,
I can't find you anywhere,
I see you inside a room,
writing something
I feel you touching my hair,
I feel your footstep in the back door,
when I want to see you,
find nothing there.
this makes me strange,
and watch the door,
with a constant stare.

SHE WILL BE COMING TO MOONSON

Relax Rafique,
the wind is gone,
but will be back,
after kissing the Himalayas,
frozen lips,
and will be gravid,
with grains of rain,
it will shower ice,
on your burning, skins,
it is monsoon,
the beautiful princess of the East,
it will be coolant,
and will spread its long, beautiful,
black hairs,
on your face and shoulders,
she will paint your desert,
with green and rainbow colors,
the buds of roses,
will germinate,
and waters will run in your,
veins and the five rivers,
She has sparkly,
lust in her hairs and eyelashes,
she is thirsty wind,
let her go, to the Himalayas,
relax Rafique,
she will be back,

as monsoon,
The oriental princess,
The beauty of Kashmir.

SILENT RAGE

You leave me lonesome
When you get apart
Silent night goes
Tangent on secretes with
Curious and audacious takeover
Resolving the mystery like a jigsaw
To end the besiege
Of molten armors, I lose the empire
Subverted throne
becomes tangled mess
A hundred suns I lived
Thousands of dreams I cherished
Faced all the aliens
Fought all the predators
Trusted my compass
Drove through all pioneering ventures
Now is the time to exhale the last fumes
The silent rage of auspicious night Is over.

SOME OLD DOMESTIC SOUNDS

I am always happy by,
winning my prospects,
and lucky also earning,
from my hobbies,
and getting respect.
asking people to swallow pills,
and making them aware of side effects,
sometimes I think a different,
and follow other assets,
I am missing some domestic sounds,
used to be having their good effects,
whoom of spinning wheel,
singing of kettle,
the hissing of an urn,
crying of children,

noise-making hens,
cows, and other pets,
and distant sounds of the steam engines,
and barking dogs,
everything gone,
now there are many caustics to the brain,
traffic noise,
and flying jets.
like old fashioned man,
I am missing comforting,
domestic sounds.

STAY WITH ME

I can see you,

when I close my eyes

when I rest on a log of a tree,

in the open sky,

and you know my sensations,

and my all blossoms,

and my old fascination,

 I'll not let you go,

I'll hold you in my dreams,

STORM IN THE CUP OF TEA

Hate when cultivated,
by defeated love,
invents,
instruments to ruin,
all with blindness,
and cold winds rush to fill,
the vacuum,
with the havoc of the storm,
ugly smiles ripple,
In face of revenge,
spitting distasteful love.
now you wake up rubbing your eyes,
someone knocking at your door.

STRANGE ENOUGH

We became two wheels of the same direction having
utmost velocity we cracked our heads by disliking

some people

I think they are watching but we never hesitate while
you put your face on my shoulder

and I caress

your beautiful hair love swings between two islands

we never cross each other's lines of defense and are
never with domestic violence wipe your tears

and remove dust from an old book read the 1st chapter
of love press my fingers gently

in your hand and smile again

SUPPOSE

Suppose that,
Love is equal to the power of sacrifice,
And the sky is blue as always,
And we are still under root,
Of two,
Suppose water is filling,
All empty spaces,
We make rains,
To empty all the clouds,
And just wipe the desert,
From all the vocabulary,
Suppose dreams are true,
As the sky is blue,
And we walk on a beach,
Arm in arm,
And no fear of weather.
and night falls on roads,
When trees look grey,
We want to stay,
In dreams prolonged to the lighthouse,
And suppose we determined,
To the never-ending story,
Of sacrifice and love.
and 1+1=1

SWEET SOULMATE

My heart and mind,
Is open for you,
and you are welcomed,
Always,
like a breezy dew,
On my eyebrows,
You are sweet,
Soul mate,
With a swing of flowers,
In thrusts of,
Whirling winds,
and hands in hands,
frozen on chilled,
Seashore,
waiting season,
Of whirling love dreams,
and singing lips,
feeling your warmth,
Infusion of your soul,
In my heart,
words are flickering,
on my lips,
Like stars,
and a bird is fluttering,
In my chest,
And as you know,
It is a glow,

TERRORISM

The voices became so silent
for the sound of bitter weeping
when the evening came
held in the flame of a candle
with the emptiness of hollow
longing like the swish of losing independence
fading in the wrap of despair
as his sword
making sibilant sound cutting
the airs wherever unconquerable mortal to do
in crowded minds full of fading desires

THE BOY WITH HIS GUITAR

Putting his little fingers,
on the strings of his guitar,
a serene boy looked to the sky,
pointed his eyes to stars,
while the night growing in dreams,
he brought his art to extremes,
and notes began floating to the heavens,
the empty silence filled all,
with sweet rhythm of his thought,
and dewdrops coming down like mists,
and musk of heavens,
soothing around,
he paused for a while,
and told me with a smile,
my mother is living with stars,
she loves my guitars,
when I play my guitar,
she makes tears of dew,
I see her in colors and hues.

THE CREATURE FROM THE HEAVENS

You are putting your eyes,
on the doors of heavens,
and want to be caressed by skies,
and you flutter,
with clouds,
and love soaring in winds,
you have no bounds,
in getting deep blood warming loves,
and putting pearls in deep blue seas,
and over the mountains,
and flow down with breezes,
while getting the glow of sunsets,
you put you your faiths and,
eternal loving face on my shoulders,
 I am to touch your cold hands,
your vibrant existence is, brightness, I am feeling,
as the skies are vast
and earth like heavens,

THE FLIGHT OF MY SOUL

Not in your streets, nor on...
your doors,
nor at your home now,
my soul flutters,
above the skies,
beneath the heavens,
in the colors of rainbows,
and in the fragrance,
of roses,
in the glitters of ice,
over the mountains,
and the gems and of pearls,
in the sea,
in the kisses of breeze,
as forever my love is getting eternal.

THE FUTURE

Past is forgotten wound,
awakened by tortures of the present,
Longing malignant hands to strangulate the future.
death leaves no flaw, In her art,
and your finished breaths with a complete,
story and replaced by new breathing baby,
that baby is your endless desire to live.,
Your image shattered into thousands,
with mirror,
And small creatures dragging their food.
Your digested dignity
runs in the blood of the crawling creatures.

THE HARVEST

My desires,
and my ambitions,
all I cherish,
and all efforts I do,
just to win,
just to have,
just to see,
a beautiful smile on your face,
that I love to see,
that is a spark,
and brightness,
of spring seasons,
I love it so much to see.

THE LINGERING GRUDGE

Like two opposite banks, of a river,
I am unable to meet and understand,
the grudge of centuries,
ruins and swamps of miserable pains
as breathing molecules of air,
with choking whispers of the
secrets of grabbed hidden cries,
coming out from the cascaded sins.
like a fire of inflamed tissues,
ending in a smoke screen,
to hide the face of offended loves,
temptation and greeds,
flowing to downtowns.
where tranquility is nailed,
on walls.,
ended fires tuned in ashes,
and smokes.
the ruler raging over
the deprives of weird conspiracy,
of rigorous faces.
The sleeping king, to love the notes,
of his flute.
and unable to find, the way out for his,
princess and prince.
making the loudest cry,
over the brim of history,
while seeing the dances,

of death.
under the red sky.

THE MERCILESS

This little world,
beneath your feet,
bringing fame to swords,
of the conquerors,
wiped the written words of fate,
from the slate of time,
and quill and strings,
on disposal of stilling verses,
while the tongue of life,
stretched to lick,
the moments of ages,
the fresh tears of the sky,
merged to fill them,
rivers of Persia,
and frozen peaks of the mountains,
saw the blood flow in their lakes,
and collusion of ages,
fuelled the tragic tales,
as the ends are always with pains,
and with mists of frozen cries,
putting the legends,
to a role on downslopes.

THE ROADS FROM THE STREETS

Some threats,
closer to necks,
distasteful to the tongue,
spitting out bitter wishes,
over the feet of patience,
pulling out the veins from.
chest of waiting hopes,
and gravid will,
spaced apart from the heart,
of walls,
street bulls heading in dark,
bruising skins with their feet,
when the milk split on dusks,
long laughed shadows,
stretching wide over the heads.
The aimless birdwatchers,
dancing on drums,
Never to see the sky,
and earthly heated, sands,
the red and hot winds,
 blowing up the cries.
now watch the silenced,
streets and sleeping doors,
out from the roads.

THE SAVAGE PURSUIT

One luke journey
Driven through cold sighs
Alternate therapy with weeds
Replenished fury
Of souls that stay in woes
Like less tender gaze of guilty
Amongst dreamers who swore
Revengeful returns
Whiningly uttered cries of hounds
breaking through the bloodshed
on the doors of prey
Screaming tense voices
Behind walls of sands
Prone to storms with desperate ascend of birds
This bitter song is a battle slogan raised
By shackled desperate who cursed his feverish life
In memories of independence inherited in posterity
As he comes down
For his sacrifice to be paid back.

THE SUNRISE

Glory is the might,
that glows over the,
cheeks of roses,
earth and moon,
 are tears of the sun,
as love is made from,
the bliss of heavens.
blood runs in the veins under,
the skin of life.
once or twice,
or always,
my heart thinks,
while beating,
if love is oceans,
waiting eyes are beach,
that adores the rising sun.

THE SURVIVAL

Life is tortured,
beyond the thresholds of painful existence,
and nature to the selection,
and squinted eye of sky,
having peripheral visibility,
deceived to outfitted exits,
and tissues fabricated,
to skeletal cages,
the inhaled stuff,
causing inflamed veils,
over the eyebrows,
of nature.
and the fittest to survive,
limping on hot stones,
of way to live.

THE WALLED CITY

Why not the cage fixer,
be punished,
and traps of hunters ruined,
and strangulating hands shackled,
the rusting flower faded,
to scorpions,
eyesight diverted to back head amnesia
walking on the barren road
eating mascarene grass
with creepy bray to pause
shrewish utters of pained revenge.
The house full of bald scalped maniacs
making louder applause.
over a rubbish demo of a stupid boss.
the feverish skulls, running to exits,
latest hells open to fools of a walled city.

THINKING OF ME

I have two ways,
one takes me towards you,
and other away from you,
and there is no wayside else,
and in between,
I am with vibrancy,
and egotistic, strengths,
where to find it?
my image,
if I am a different,
I think sometimes,
for and about me.

THIS NIGHT

Dancing and hallucinating, fireflies,
behind the blinded, thoughts,
lost in gravities of straying ideas
in void spaces of thick blood,
sticking on walls of ages,
nauseous like whirling dervish,
and stupor of metamorphosis,
maggot-like larva sticking,
on the tongue of a beautiful virgin
 of time and space.
my loved planet is broken,
into astroids,
and fates and lucks,
smoked to ends,
closing the eyes of the sky.
clouds are reluctant to,
exhale their vapors, on my palms,
green leaves ripening,
beneath my eyebrows,
wet with dewdrops

TIDES OF THE TIME

Long long staring eyes,
frozen eternity to real,
t may be so valid,
like the rising sun of the east
While few feet beneath my feet,
there is another world,
dormant and silent,
like lips of the bride,
time jumps too long,
Enslaving the moments in the cage,
Your presence is worthy,
Leaving me in a slot,
I may think a lot,
to untie this knot,

TRIPLE PURPLE ANGELS TRUMPET

My veiled desires pouring,
out of my veins,
and my mutant genes,
germinating in grooves,
of moist brick walls,
of alley,
making stalks of weeds,
my four chambers,
of heart throwing my red,
and white cells out of windows,
there is a breed of multiple,
disorders of personality,
a tornado of psychotropic pills,
over-aggressive, cries,
of wisdom in darkened insanity,
roses crushed beneath,
eet of aggravated pains,
the angels' breathless in veins,
it is numbness, of sorrow,
suffocated, lulled,
a rumble of judgment day,
the sun is coming down,
the winds are to blow up,
everything,
coming from,
triple purple angel's trumpet

TURBULENCE

This time difference,
marking stillbirths stories,
related to extinguished generations.
 ruling for centuries,
watching with graves of kings.
and their fish mouth shaped, crowns,
telling the tale of cruelty,
and darkened shadows,
dancing over their skulls.
the days are not other than,
when the peace was set on ablaze,
and life riddled with calamities,
the surface of the earth pained with inflamed desires.
when the ages quickened in hands,
leaving running out astonishments to humanity.

UNCERTAIN BREATHS

It was all about,
and some mishap,
we walked through unpaved,
road of life.
and our aches,
pretended to smile, when,
Joined hand to hand,
In the stream of pains,
rolling like uprooted bush,
Pushed by fated winds,
Longing up to nominal stare
and the journey ends with strides,
chocking whispered cries.,
was it some unfamiliar gaze? ,
while soul and body,
Just broken,
on a pause of breaths, ...
....
so uncertain breaths.

UNFORGETTABLE

Is anything wrong?
I don't think anything went wrong,
we lived as a family,
in a dreamland,
we made a long drive in the rain and open sky,
we floated in dreams,
I think you got beautiful moments,
foolproof and open-hearted,
my hands were soothing,
it was what I can't understand,
and you also,
if you miss this union,
then it was love,
if you have forgotten,
it was a miraculous imagination,
if you still don't understand,
then it is eternal love.
you found it accidentally,

Victims

Sorrowful cries and wails fallen
behind your brick wall and dying
flame of desire fluttering at your door
with tears
on each fragment of memories
declare the independence
 from life with scattered tissues
in a pool of blood
this sizzling evening is different
than every mournful event
as innocents are slain by ruthless claws
again telling the peacekeepers
the undeclared war of evil is not over

VIRTUAL HARASSMENTS

My image broken,
with my mirror image,
shattered into millions of pixels,
mine living tissues under a spell,
of visual acuity,
reflective trouble-shooters,
 parallel index,
nevertheless it all nothing,
virtual harassment,
a weapon of future war,
bloodless bloodshed changed,
reshaped, sharpened threats,
hunting
slavery child abuse,
painful labor,
unskiled roundups, wars,
only survival,
condition to surrender,
before the invisible enemy.

VOICE OF LOVE

Some serene words on your lips
wise to listen in long silence of my soul
offer your kind mood to favor
the blossoms that woke up
my slowly dying ambition I learned to soar
despite the season as I could dare
to unfold my tied wings
let my wings brush the breeze and clouds to bow
on the rainbow
and stars to scatter in my dreams
and charms of the spring kisses to glow with roses
and solitude of journey in raining love
to glimmer with occasional sunshine
likely my first kiss
to your memory of love
might be awaiting the heavenly bliss
as I walk on roads
bare feet to reach your voice of love

VOID DAY

It was a sexually thrust,
and over-aggressive stare of the sky,
rendering skull bones detached,
likely torn thought,
murmuring like flies over,
 rancid grapes,
dragging my legs over thorn of time,
 teasing sounds pierced my ear saccules,
 motive....to aware my soul,
from hot glazes of the sun.
one splash of water wetting my eyes,
who could be the food of
wild velociraptors,
they need their hunger,
exaggerated with promises,
of proteins,
dribbled saliva showing their tactful hunting,
Radar and bullet useless,
with fused batteries,
I am to run back with an angel,
from the warfare,
of dream

WAITING ALWAYS

All I wanted to know was,
what you don't prettily tell,
either me next to recollect,
the crusts of mine wounds underneath,
or my heart sounds aloud,
awakening from the sleep,
and wandering clouds,
to see from the window,
over the distant white mountain
in the fully growing moon,
like a sleeping bird in his nest.
to open sky,
my eyes waiting,
and dancing flaws in clouds,
making unrest aloud lightening
in a sheath of open heart,
I am feeling your face in my hands,
I see my face your eyes,
 but there is getting silence,
in my ears, your voices raising,
from my thoughts,
that linger like smoke in still air,
and my frozen hopes, suspended in the room,
and a door opens I see you, coming in,
it always seems to be,
 it is always a dream for me,
but it goes on, till morning. every night

WAITING IN THE WINGS

When the roads,
streets and trees of the,
the city is asleep,
I am with empty arms,
before the silence of my room,
and waiting with a constant stare,
 on drowsy LCD of my PC,
with my vestige wings,
wanting to fly some island,
with mine sclerotic heart,
kisses and hugs soaring in thoughts,
and floating on the sea of,
visionary bands of love,
I see white doves coming down,
from higher clouds,
and the moon hiding behind pieces
of clouds with a circled hollow of brightness,
nights are not always dressed,
with kindness,
and fragrance of jasmines,
not always mine,
until dreams are real,
and getting bliss of life.

WALK HAND IN HAND

A silent procession walking through a garden
Speaks the dreams, ambitions
And things that can't be undone
Infestation of daydreams
That fade with rolling in the night
There are finally footsteps
To be heard softly upon the stone stair
we walked through the winters
Fallen leaves and scattered dead grasses
Unable to numb our feelings
Was it a fearless agony?
Or we crossed a line
On a journey measuring the hours
Of untold history
Even we don't understand the mysteries of life
Straying in the fissures of oblivion
We walk hand in hand.

WALKING WITH WILD AMNESIA

You blew rose petals,
 on your palm,
went floating in the air,
simulating butterflies in circles.
we went walking slowly on flowered,
paths, of life,
to the love dreams,
searching snails on the beach,
over footprints of birds,
the crimson rays of the setting sun
passing through your golden hair.
 your lips paused saying something,
 you wanted to say,
putting your face on my heart,
my fingers touching your eyelashes,
and crossing the arches of eyebrows,
forgetting myself,
got lost in your green eyes lakes,
 and you went too deep sleep,
in my open arms.
golden water ran over the words
written on the sands,
our promises slowly grew in the daydreams.
our souls diffused in eternity,
and the snow spreading on the earth,
chilled to the core of existence.
and finally was goodbye,

leaving your warm tears on my palms,
I am standing under an autumn tree,
listening to the crying withered leaves under my feet.
Gems never remain,
always with us, the parents,
the vigor's of the youth age loving friends,
and singing birds of the springs.
I am alone walking on the barren road of life
with my wild amnesia.

WALLS

You are right, I know this,
since I never knew,
anything about my whereabouts,
when objectives flamed,
in smokes,
and strains pierced,
blistering ambitions,
predatory weathers,
prevailed on roofs,
and pyramids rose on sands,
when humanity was shackled,
and scales were invented,
to weigh the mass value of blood and water,
and flesh was fuelled,
to raise walls,

WELCOME BACK

Glitters of our bonds,

 got rusted with time,

You got changed a little, and me also,

like winds,

and moving ocean, we are alive,

with healed scars, we are back,

on the road of life,

with the same passions,

as these were before,

WHEN YOU ARE COMING?

I am here with love,
 sympathetic neurons,
 peaceful dreams,
What remains,
Is a bunch of roses,
and breezily love,
waiting for your advent,
doors of my eyes opened in silence,
of nights, and colors, of days,
the walls of my home standing still,
 on toes of hopes,
the trees of my garden,
 are bowing with fruits,
and full moon with his duties,
 Star is flickering,
with notes of string.,
weathers are springs for you,
don't change your destiny,
at this place,
You're strange,
desires are welcomed here.

WHERE THE SUN SETS

In the lap of the horizon,
over the blinks of the evening lulls,
red yellow and crimson clouds,
the painted sky by the greater sun,
a canvas of love & faith,
a bride of the universe,
with a red glow on her face,
and a kiss of orange on her lips,
always with golden hair and bliss,
pride of the whole day,
the evening sky with sunset.
the golden grass and golden trees,
 and longing shadows towards the ends and birds
flying back to their nests,

always it is out of reach,
always want to go there,
where there the sun sets.

WHILE I SMILE

The smile on my face,
is not a possible truth,
I may not tell you, what I feel,
my wounds are never to heal,
What I should reveal,
and what should I conceal,
Lingers a question,
In my eyes,
and writes a wrinkle,
On my face,
till the ends are far-reaching,
and hope that peeps,
like oozing blood from the skin,
The real hides deeper than that.,
and you stay in front of me,
to make doubts,
about me, and my person,
while I am talking.

WHY TO MISS?

If you got my taste,
then why to waste,
 the time in your fist,
running so swift,
and don't think,
a bird in the sky,
that will fly,
and never be shy,
Or you will cry, and why,
you are too late?
 to know your fate.

WILD MISADVENTURE

Sparrows are falling,
like stones,
from the sky,
over the clouds,
the baby is hungry,
swallowing the paper,
no more teething,
mum is sneezing,
virtual virus,
just now breeding,
in my nightmare,
elephant foot,
stepping on my chest,
no more crying,
event for to die,
I am here,
and nowhere,
 what to share,
just my life,
coming soon,
on the moon,
purple baboon,
seen from here,
how you dare,
don't stare,
it's unfair,
no more eyes,

eyes of tiger,
fixed over my face,
needled canines,
on my jaws,
I can eat,
all your meat,
all your flesh all your skin,
born to win,
don't fear, I am alone,
 just come down,
without your gun

WITHOUT LOVE

Without your love,
I am just a plant of chili,
with brittle buds,
and barren futures,
darker nights,
scorching days,
haunted mind,
opaque eyes,
 parched lips,
 drunken gaits,
half-hearted motives,
useless gestures.
pointless thoughts,
and nothing else.

WOLVES ARE SILENT

The time might have worn out my memories
Had not any stubborn circumstance
Required courage to overcome fears
There are nights when wolves are silent
Howling is still mysterious in the mountains
That walks alone with stars
With a disturbed sense of sight and sound
Can stray in weary waysides
As Illusions look very real
Dear moonlight
These are only my memories
That disturbs my nights
Since you invite me
To see roses in your garden
 Where stars are darting their rays
The dream is not over
I absolutely adore you, my dear
Will you bless me with tomorrow
 That will be coming with the sun
As you live in the center of my thoughts
 I am walking down memory lane.

WORN-OUT BLOOMS

A withering leaf,
Crestfallen,
Below the clouds of sorrow,
Waiting for the loud lightning,
To jump down,
In depths of saddened, end,
And slow moonlight,
prevailing behind the darkness,
of rainy clouds,
waiting for the kiss of heavens.
And banks of a river,
Standing silent with questions.
Is it a clear fate?
To find empty hands,
Where worn-out blooms,
 End in glooms

WRITTEN TRUTH

Under the shadow of,
your eyelashes,
Tears blink in agony,
And daffodils dancing,
With vibrant lips,
Pain floats with notes,
making a scratch on the heart,
The glow on cheeks,
Is oozing love.
I am smiling over,
Knots of strange moments,
You are so beautiful.

YOUR AUDLEY IMAGE

My heart flutters for you,
more as you are a dream,
or reality,
or still a stranger,
or a question about unseen realities,
may I look,
my face in your words,
 somewhere,
written on a wall of, sands,
in the desert of fate,
or footprints,
mine that leads to,
 the search for my desire,
or my famous despairs.
 born with ill-fated,
person of me,
mingled to strive for,
 my viability,
righteous to live,
on audible hopes.

DR. MUHAMMAD RAFIQUE FAROOQI

Date of birth: 22 April 1959

I was born in district Gujranwala Pakistan, I matriculated from govt. High School Qilla Didar Singh, FSc from Government College LAHORE: and MBBS from Allama Iqbal Medical College Lahore: in 1984, I am doing my G.P practices, at Lahore, Writing is my Hobby.